Before You Speak

Lessons that I wish I had known before filing a whistleblower case against the Department of Veterans Affairs

Acknowledgments

To my wife and kids: You are my shelter, my sound of reason, and my source of safety. Without you, I am not sure how I would handle this storm. Your unwavering support gives me the strength to face each day, and for that, I am eternally grateful.

By D.M.

Chapter Index

- **Chapter 1: The Personal Costs**
    - Whistleblowing
    - Emotional Toll on Whistleblowers
    - Feelings of isolation and betrayal are common
    - Impact on Family and Personal Life
    - Financial struggles are another significant consequence
    - Mental Health Effects and Anxiety
    - Stories and Testimonies from VA Whistleblowers
- **Chapter 2: Professional Repercussions**
    - Career Risks and Challenges in Finding Future Employment
    - The Reality of Blacklisting
    - Isolation and the Loss of Professional Relationships
    - Examples from VA Cases

- Discussion on VA Internal Policies
- **Chapter 3: Legal Challenges**
  - The Cost of Courage
  - The Whistleblower Protection Act (WPA) and Whistleblower Protection Enhancement Act (WPEA)
  - The Labyrinth of Legal Battles
  - Fighting for Integrity While Facing Financial Ruin
  - Case Studies: David vs. Goliath
  - The Importance of Legal Reform
  - Conclusion
- **Chapter 4: The Sting of Retaliation**
  - Definition and Forms of Retaliation
  - Institutional Retaliation within the VA
  - The Isolation Effect
  - Personal Anecdote
  - Legal Protections and Strategies for Mitigating Retaliation
  - Conclusion

- **Chapter 5: The Role of the Office of Accountability and Whistleblower Protection (OAWP)**
  - Assessment of the Effectiveness of the OAWP
  - Testimonies from Whistleblowers about Their Experiences with the OAWP
  - Limitations and Challenges Faced by the OAWP
  - Conclusion
- **Chapter 6: Coping Mechanisms and Support Systems**
  - Psychological Support and Counseling
  - Support Networks and Advocacy Groups
  - Strategies for Maintaining Resilience and Well-Being
  - Conclusion
- **Chapter 7: Policy Recommendations and Future Directions**
  - Recommendations for Strengthening Whistleblower Protections
  - Future Directions for VA Policies and Practices
  - Concluding Thoughts on the Need for Systemic Change

Introduction: Before You Speak

When people think of whistleblowing, it's often painted as a noble and courageous act where the truth prevails, and justice is served. However, for those who have walked this path, particularly within the Department of Veterans Affairs (VA), the reality is far more complex and fraught with peril. Whistleblowing is not merely a professional risk; it's a personal sacrifice with profound and often devastating ramifications.

Stepping into the Storm

Deciding to blow the whistle on misconduct within the VA is akin to stepping into a storm. When you raise your voice, you may find yourself quickly marginalized, your credibility questioned, and your motives scrutinized. The institution you aim to protect can become an adversary, setting you up for failure and subjecting you to rigorous scrutiny.

Isolation becomes a constant companion. Colleagues who once were friends may distance themselves, fearing that association with a whistleblower could jeopardize their careers. The sense of betrayal and abandonment can be overwhelming, intensifying the emotional and psychological toll.

The Battle for Belief

Not being believed is another harsh reality. The institution may rally its forces to discredit you, portraying you as a disgruntled employee or an unreliable narrator. Your claims, no matter how substantiated, could be met with skepticism, and the burden of proof falls squarely on your shoulders. Retaliation can be subtle or overt, but it is almost always relentless. You might be set up for failure through impossible tasks, unreasonable deadlines, or a lack of necessary resources. Performance-based actions, disciplinary measures, and even attempts to remove you from federal service can follow in quick

Succession. The aim is clear: to silence you, to break your resolve, and to make an example of you to deter others from following in your footsteps.

Navigating a Complex Web of Legal Protections

The VA has a range of rules and policies aimed at protecting those who report misconduct. Key among these are the Whistleblower Protection Act (WPA) and the Whistleblower Protection Enhancement Act (WPEA), both designed to guard federal employees from retaliation. However, these laws are not always as effective as they appear. The regulations can be overwhelming, forming a confusing maze that whistleblowers must carefully navigate.

Take, for instance, the VA Handbook 5021, which outlines how disciplinary actions should be handled. Yet, in some cases historically have failed to follow these directives However, this same handbook has been used to target whistleblowers, disguised as performance or conduct issues. Similarly, the Office of Accountability and Whistleblower Protection (OAWP) was created to offer support, but many have found it lacking, with reports of insufficient staffing and funding.

Adding to the challenge, the Merit Systems Protection Board (MSPB), which handles whistleblower complaints, has faced significant delays, leaving whistleblowers stuck without a timely resolution. These bureaucratic hurdles often discourage individuals from speaking out, knowing that the system may not be on their side.

Revealing the Hidden Costs

This book sheds light on the often-unseen costs of whistleblowing within the VA. We will explore the personal, professional, legal, and emotional consequences faced by those who choose to speak up. Using real-life examples, legal perspectives, and personal stories, we aim to expose the sacrifices these courageous individuals make and allow you to judge whether it's a risk worth taking in your career.

This isn't just a narrative about the hardships of coming forward. It's a call to acknowledge and support those who bravely choose to shine a light on the truth, even when faced with overwhelming challenges. The path is difficult, but it's a journey that needs to be understood, respected, and protected—or perhaps avoided to preserve one's career.

The Importance of This Book

As you move through these pages, take a moment to reflect on the tremendous courage it takes to stand up against an institution as large and influential as the VA. The people whose stories fill this book did so at great personal risk—not for attention, but to make sure that the truth is heard, and that the VA remains accountable to the veterans it serves.

Whether you're thinking about becoming a whistleblower, supporting someone who is, or simply seeking to understand the intricate dynamics involved, this book serves as a guide. By exposing the hidden costs of whistleblowing, our goal is to foster a deeper awareness of the sacrifices involved and highlight the need for better protection and support systems for those who make this brave choice.

Whistleblowing is not for the faint of heart. It is a journey of resilience, determination, and unwavering moral integrity. I hope that this book will provide you with the knowledge, insights, and courage to make the best decision for yourself, your career, and the veterans you serve.

Chapter 1: The Personal Costs

Whistleblowing

Whistleblowing is an act that brings unethical, illegal, or improper behavior to light, often by employees who hope to correct these wrongs by reporting them to those in power. This demands deep moral courage within the intricate structure of the Veterans Affairs (VA) system, whistleblowers hold a crucial position. They act as sentinels of integrity, revealing issues that might otherwise stay hidden. However, this honorable role comes with significant personal sacrifices.

Emotional Toll on Whistleblowers

The emotional burden borne by whistleblowers is staggering. The decision to report wrongdoing is not taken lightly; it is accompanied by a maelstrom of stress and anxiety. Whistleblowers are often besieged by fears of retaliation, uncertainty about the outcomes, and the looming specter of ostracism by colleagues and superiors. This emotional tempest can lead to severe psychological distress.

Feelings of isolation and betrayal

The workplace, once a sanctuary of camaraderie and support, can transform into a hostile environment. Colleagues may distance themselves out of fear or pressure from leadership, leaving the whistleblower to navigate a landscape of loneliness and abandonment. This emotional isolation can be devastating, compounding mental strain. Dr. Katherine Mitchell's harrowing experience provides a poignant illustration. As a former VA whistleblower, Dr. Mitchell exposed systemic issues within the Phoenix VA Health Care System, including patient care delays that led to preventable deaths. In the aftermath, she faced severe professional isolation and attempts to discredit her. The emotional toll was profound, leading to overwhelming stress and anxiety that permeated every facet of her life.

Effect on Family and Personal Life

The consequences of whistleblowing often ripple beyond the individual, deeply affecting their family and personal life. The stress and anxiety that whistleblowers carry inevitably can impact their home, putting strain on relationships with loved ones. Marriages may suffer, parenting becomes more challenging, and the family's overall well-being can deteriorate.

Financial struggles are another significant consequence

Retaliation can lead to demotions, pay cuts, or job loss, resulting in financial hardship. Legal battles that follow can be drawn out and costly, draining family resources and increasing stress. The story of Brandon Coleman highlights these personal costs. As a whistleblower who revealed critical issues related to the treatment of suicidal veterans, Coleman faced severe retaliation, including suspension and threats of termination. The financial and emotional toll of these actions weighed heavily on his family, illustrating the far-reaching effects of his brave decisions.

Mental Health Effects and Anxiety

The impact on mental health for whistleblowers can be profound. Persistent anxiety, fueled by fears of retaliation and uncertainty about what lies ahead, often becomes a constant burden. This ongoing stress may result in insomnia, depression, and, in some cases, even thoughts of self-harm. For some, the emotional toll becomes unbearable, leading them to seek an escape from the overwhelming pressure.

Additionally, whistleblowers frequently find themselves in a heightened state of alertness, always looking over their shoulders during ordinary tasks. The fear of being followed, monitored, or harassed can lead to consume paranoia, which only worsens their mental state.

Stories and Testimonies from VA Whistleblowers

Firsthand accounts provide a powerful window into the personal toll of whistleblowing. These stories emphasize the courage it takes to step forward, along with the deep sacrifices made by whistleblowers and their families.

- Dr. Katherine Mitchell: "The emotional weight was crushing. I felt abandoned by my colleagues, and the stress took a toll on my health and my family life. Still, I knew I had to speak up for the veterans who were being harmed."
- Brandon Coleman: "The retaliation was relentless. I faced suspension, and threats of termination, and my family struggled financially. But I couldn't stay quiet when veterans' lives were on the line."

- Paula Pedene: As a public affairs officer at Phoenix VA, Pedene revealed financial mismanagement and suffered significant retaliation, including being reassigned to menial work and professional isolation. "The stress was overwhelming, affecting every part of my life. But I had to do what was right."

These testimonies underscore the severe personal costs associated with whistleblowing. The emotional and psychological toll, coupled with the impact on family and personal life, highlights the immense bravery of those who choose to speak out.

Notes:

Chapter 2: Professional Repercussions

Career Risks and Challenges in Finding Future Employment

Whistleblowing, while a courageous act, often comes with significant professional repercussions. The decision to expose wrongdoing can jeopardize one's career, leading to demotions, terminations, and an indelible mark on one's professional reputation. Whistleblowers are frequently ostracized within their organizations and branded as troublemakers or disloyal employees. This stigma can make it exceedingly difficult to find future employment, as potential employers may view whistleblowers as a liability or fear that they may bring similar scrutiny to their new workplace.

One of the most challenging aspects for whistleblowers is the potential for career derailment. The retaliation they face often manifests in punitive measures such as demotion, reassignment to less desirable positions, or even termination. These steps not only affect their current job status but can also hinder their professional growth and advancement. Professional isolation and stigmatization can be career-ending, leaving whistleblowers with limited opportunities and tarnished professional reputations.

The Reality of Blacklisting

Being blacklisted is a genuine challenge for whistleblowers. Once someone is labeled as a whistleblower, finding employment within their industry can become almost impossible. Hiring managers may view whistleblowers as high-risk, fearing they might uncover future problems within their organization. This stigma can result in extended periods of unemployment or even force whistleblowers to seek new career paths altogether.

Isolation and the Loss of Professional Relationships

The professional repercussions extend beyond career

opportunities: whistleblowers often experience profound isolation. Colleagues who were once friends may distance themselves, fearing association with someone perceived as a troublemaker. This social ostracization can be incredibly isolating, making the whistleblower feel like they always have a target on their back.

The loss of professional relationships and support networks exacerbates the stress and anxiety associated with whistleblowing. The sense of being continuously watched or targeted can create a hostile work environment, contributing to a decline in mental health and overall well-being.

Examples from VA Cases

The experiences of VA whistleblowers highlight the severe professional repercussions they endure.

- These cases provide a sobering reminder of the risks involved in exposing wrongdoing within the

- VA system.

    Dr. Katherine Mitchell: A physician at the Phoenix VA Health Care System, Dr. Mitchell brought attention to serious patient care issues, such as long wait times and poor medical treatment. In response to her disclosures, she faced retaliation, including being removed from her clinical duties and reassigned to administrative roles that severely limited her ability to practice medicine. Additionally, her colleagues distanced themselves, making her feel unsupported, isolated, and targeted.

- **Joseph Colon**: A former employee at the Puerto Rico VA, Colon reported concerns about corruption and mismanagement. After speaking out, he experienced harsh retaliation, including suspension and threats of termination. His reputation suffered, making it hard to find employment elsewhere. He was effectively blacklisted in his field, and colleagues who had previously supported him began to avoid him.

- **Jamie Fox**: A nurse at the VA Medical Center in Cincinnati, Fox reported unsafe patient care practices and faced retaliatory actions, which included reassignment to less favorable shifts and roles. These actions damaged her professional reputation, created significant personal and financial strain, and left her feeling isolated in a hostile work environment.

As stated, these cases illustrate the profound professional risks and challenges faced by VA whistleblowers. Their experiences underscore the need for robust protections and support systems to safeguard the careers of those who speak out against wrongdoing.

Notes:

Chapter 3: Legal Challenges

The Cost of Courage

The Cost of Courage Imagine being a VA employee who uncovers widespread wrongdoing. You are left with a difficult choice: stay quiet and let the issues persist or speak out, knowing you could lose everything. This was the situation for Lisa, a nurse at a VA hospital who was exposed to serious patient care problems. Motivated by her dedication to veterans' health, Lisa blew the whistle. This decision would change her life dramatically. She soon faced hostility from her supervisors and colleagues, and her work environment became intolerable. Formal disciplinary actions followed without warning, affecting her mental and emotional well-being. The legal challenges she encountered, however, were just as overwhelming.

The Whistleblower Protection Act (WPA) of 1989 and the Whistleblower Protection Enhancement Act (WPEA) of 2012 are designed to shield federal employees from retaliation. These laws provide a framework for whistleblowers to report misconduct without fear of reprisal. However, the reality is often far more complicated. The WPA and WPEA stipulate that whistleblowers should not face adverse consequences for their disclosures. They include provisions for legal recourse, such as the right to appeal retaliatory actions and seek remedies through the U.S. Office of Special Counsel (OSC). However, navigating these legal waters requires significant time, resources, and resilience. The labyrinth of legal battles for Lisa, invoking these protections was just the beginning of a long and arduous journey. She filed a complaint with the OSC, hoping for swift justice. Instead, she found herself entangled in a complicated process that demanded extensive documentation, legal knowledge, and financial resources she did not have. Legal battles can be prohibitively expensive, and many whistleblowers, like Lisa, find themselves at a stark disadvantage. They often face well-funded legal teams representing the VA, making the fight for justice feel like an uphill battle. The financial strain can be crippling, as whistleblowers may need to hire legal representatives, take time off work, or even lose their jobs entirely. Fighting for integrity while facing financial ruin is not unique for most who come forward.

The struggle to maintain one's integrity while facing overwhelming legal and financial pressures is a common theme among VA whistleblowers. When Lisa lost her job, her financial situation became dire. Without a steady income, she could no longer afford the legal representation needed to continue her fight. The VA, on the other hand, had ample resources to deploy multiple lawyers, crafting a narrative that painted Lisa in a negative light. These legal teams often employ tactics designed to discredit whistleblowers, scrutinizing their personal and professional lives for any inconsistencies or vulnerabilities. In Lisa's case, minor errors in her extensive documentation were blown out of proportion, and her motives were questioned at every turn. The emotional and financial toll was devastating, leaving her feeling isolated and powerless.

Case Studies: David vs. Goliath several high-profile cases illustrate the severe legal challenges faced by VA whistleblowers. Take the case of Dr. James Mitchell, who testified before the House Committee on Veterans Affairs in 2015. Dr. Mitchell exposed fraudulent scheduling practices that endangered patients' lives. Despite the protections theoretically afforded by the WPA and WPEA, he endured years of legal battles, professional ostracization, and personal hardship.

Similarly, Jamie Fox, a VA nurse, faced relentless retaliation after speaking out about patient care issues. In an interview with NBC News, she recounted how her life was turned upside down by continuous legal struggles, the emotional toll of standing up against a powerful institution, and the importance of legal reform. These stories underscore the urgent need for stronger legal protection and reform. While the WPA and WPEA provide a framework, their enforcement and practical application often fall short and are considered the status quo. Whistleblowers need more accessible legal resources, faster resolution processes, and comprehensive support systems to ensure their voices are heard without devastating personal consequences. Not a system that sends you in different directions, only to advise you after months of waiting that you need to try a different office altogether.

Conclusion

The legal challenges faced by VA whistleblowers like Lisa, Dr. Mitchell, and Jamie Fox highlight the immense courage required to stand up against wrongdoing. Their stories are a testament to the resilience of those who prioritize integrity and justice over personal safety and stability. However, they also reveal significant gaps in the current legal framework that must be addressed to protect these brave individuals.

Without adequate financial and legal support, whistleblowers are left vulnerable and isolated, often feeling as if they are fighting a losing battle against a system designed to protect the status quo. The current legal framework, as embodied by the WPA and WPEA, is a step in the right direction but remains insufficient in practice. The labyrinthine legal processes, the financial burdens, and the emotional toll create a formidable barrier that many whistleblowers cannot overcome.

Comprehensive reforms are needed to honor the bravery of individuals like Lisa, Dr. Mitchell, and Jamie Fox. These reforms should include enhanced legal protections that are not only robust on paper but also readily enforceable. Faster resolution mechanisms, financial assistance for independent legal representation, and stronger safeguards against retaliation are essential components of an improved system.

Moreover, creating a culture within the VA that genuinely values transparency and accountability is crucial. This involves not only policy changes but also a shift in organizational ethos, where whistleblowers are seen as allies in the pursuit of excellence rather than as threats to be neutralized.

In conclusion, while the stories of VA whistleblowers paint a grim picture of the current legal landscape, they also serve as a powerful call to action. The courage and integrity displayed by these individuals demands a response that goes beyond acknowledgment—it requires decisive and meaningful legal reform. Only then can we ensure that whistleblowers are protected, their voices amplified, and the systems they seek to improve are held accountable for the betterment of all.

Notes:

Chapter 4: The Sting of Retaliation

Definition and Forms of Retaliation

Retaliation is the punishment faced by those who report illegal or unethical activities. Within the VA, this can take many forms, such as:

Demotions and Job Reassignments Scare tactics of demotion and being moved to less desirable roles could be a direct consequence of speaking out. This not only damages their professional reputation but also serves as a warning to others in the organization.

Harassment and Bullying Whistleblowers may endure hostile work environments, including bullying, threats, or being socially excluded by coworkers and supervisors. Harassment can be subtle, like being left out of meetings, or more obvious, such as public reprimands.

Unfair Performance Reviews Whistleblowers might receive overly negative performance evaluations, making it harder for them to advance in their careers. These reviews can also be used as justification for further disciplinary actions or even termination.

Being Fired In extreme cases, whistleblowers may lose their jobs under the guise of "performance issues". "restructuring" or "conduct."

Retaliation within the VA is not just a matter of individual action; it can be institutionalized, affecting the entire organizational culture. Veterans Affairs, being one of the largest federal agencies, has a complex bureaucracy that can sometimes be weaponized against whistleblowers. Several high-profile cases have highlighted systemic issues, including:

- Dr. Katherine Mitchell: Dr. Mitchell, a VA physician, faced retaliation after exposing inadequacies in emergency care at the Phoenix VA Health Care System. She experienced harassment, was removed from her position, and her work environment became increasingly hostile.

- Dr. Jose Mathews: Dr. Mathews, chief of psychiatry, reported underperformance in patient care at the St. Louis VA Health Care System. Subsequently, he was demoted and isolated from his colleagues, illustrating a clear pattern of institutional retaliation. The isolation effects are one of the most insidious forms of retaliation, where whistleblowers are systematically ostracized by their colleagues and supervisors. This isolation can be deeply damaging, both professionally and personally, as it creates an environment where the whistleblower feels abandoned and unsupported. VA's organizational culture, which emphasizes improvement and a just culture, paradoxically can turn hostile when negative information is brought to light throwing away the forms taught from day one of orientation with new employees who enter federal service.

Colleagues and supervisors may:

Withhold Support Whistleblowers may find that the support they previously enjoyed from supervisors and peers is withdrawn, leaving them to navigate their challenges alone.

Spread Negative Rumors In some cases, efforts are made to discredit the whistleblower through rumors and gossip, further eroding their professional standing and personal relationships. This cultural phenomenon is deeply embedded within the VA, where the organization often mobilizes its resources, power, and finances to discredit those who expose its flaws. This institutional behavior underscores the immense personal costs that whistleblowers endure, highlighting the need for robust protective measures.

Personal Anecdote

In my own experience, retaliation took a particularly damaging form. A colleague actively refused to gather and present information that would exonerate me and bring the truth to light. Instead, she deceived the attorneys involved in my case with misinformation. This betrayal not only impacted my professional standing but also caused significant emotional distress. The isolation and misinformation campaign orchestrated by this colleague exemplifies the lengths to which individuals within the VA may go to protect their careers and align with the institutional agenda, even at the cost of justice and integrity.

Legal Protections and Strategies for Mitigating Retaliation

Despite the pervasive nature of retaliation, several legal frameworks are designed to protect whistleblowers. Key among these are the Whistleblower Protection Act (WPA) and the Whistleblower Protection

Enhancement Act (WPEA). These laws allow whistleblowers to seek redress and offer protection against retaliatory actions.

Whistleblower Protection Act (WPA) Enacted in 1989, the WPA aims to protect federal employees who disclose evidence of illegal or improper government activities. It prohibits retaliatory actions against whistleblowers and provides avenues for filing complaints with the Office of Special Counsel (OSC).

Whistleblower Protection Enhancement Act (WPEA) The WPEA, an extension of the WPA enacted in 2012, strengthens protections for whistleblowers by addressing loopholes and expanding the scope of protections.

Strategies for Mitigating Retaliation

While legal protections are crucial, whistleblowers can also adopt strategies to mitigate retaliation:

Documentation: Maintain detailed records of all communications and incidents related to whistleblowing can serve as critical evidence in legal proceedings.

Seeking Support Engaging with whistleblower protection organizations, legal counsel, and support networks can provide essential guidance and moral support.

Understanding Rights Awareness of one's legal rights and the procedures for reporting retaliation can empower whistleblowers to take appropriate actions.

Conclusion

Retaliation remains a significant deterrent for potential whistleblowers within the VA. Despite the risks, legal frameworks such as the WPA and WPEA provide robust protection. By understanding the forms of retaliation and leveraging available legal and support mechanisms, whistleblowers can navigate the challenges and continue their vital role in ensuring accountability within the VA.

Notes:

Chapter 5: The Role of the Office of Accountability and Whistleblower Protection (OAWP)

Assessment of the Effectiveness of the OAWP

The Office of Accountability and Whistleblower Protection (OAWP) was created to provide a safe channel for whistleblowers to report misconduct without fear of retaliation. It aims to foster a culture of transparency and accountability within the VA. However, the effectiveness of the OAWP has been a subject of debate. Some whistleblowers have found the OAWP to be an invaluable resource, while others have faced significant obstacles.

Testimonies from Whistleblowers about Their Experiences with the OAWP

- Dr. Katherine Mitchell: "The OAWP was supposed to be my ally, but I often felt like they were another hurdle to overcome. While they provided some support, the process was slow and bureaucratic."

- Brandon Coleman: "The OAWP gave me a platform to voice my concerns, but the lack of timely action made it feel like an uphill battle. Their intentions are good, but the execution needs improvement."

Limitations and Challenges Faced by the OAWP

The OAWP faces several challenges that hinder its effectiveness:

Understaffing and Underfunding: The OAWP is often understaffed and underfunded, limiting its ability to thoroughly investigate all cases.

Bureaucratic Delays The process of addressing complaints can be slow, causing frustration for whistleblowers who seek timely resolutions.

Perceived Bias Some whistleblowers perceive the OAWP as being biased towards the VA, questioning the impartiality of investigations. The same internal offices are looped back into the complaints and have a heavy hand in the influence of the outcome, so the bias of this is not in your favor.

Conclusion The OAWP plays a crucial role in protecting whistleblowers and ensuring accountability within the VA. However, to truly fulfill its mission, the OAWP must address its limitations and enhance its support for whistleblowers. Strengthening the office through increased staffing, funding, and streamlined processes can help build trust, Moreover, political unbiased encourages more whistleblowers to come forward.

In my personal experience, the hurdles one must navigate are often the polar opposite of what is advertised. Agencies that promise responses within a specific time frame often leave you waiting indefinitely: no letters, no emails, and no calls. Instead, you find yourself bouncing around in an endless Rolodex, faced with canceled appointments or no-shows. The system feels as though it's designed to confuse and make you give up. These outcomes seem preplanned, and many lawyers, aware of this reality, still take the risk, knowing the challenges their clients will inevitably face a negative outcome.

Notes:

Chapter 6: Coping Mechanisms and Support Systems

Psychological Support and Counseling

Whistleblowers typically experience significant stress, anxiety, and emotional turmoil. Access to psychological support and counseling is essential for their mental health. Therapy can provide a safe space to process emotions and develop coping strategies. Professional counseling can also help mitigate the risk of long-term psychological damage, such as chronic stress, depression, or PTSD.

Support Networks and Advocacy Groups

Connecting with support networks and advocacy organizations can be a great source of moral support and practical guidance. Groups like the Government Accountability Project (GAP) and the National Whistleblower Center (NWC) provide resources, legal advice, and connections with other whistleblowers who have faced similar challenges. These organizations also advocate for whistleblowers, helping to raise awareness about systemic issues and amplify their voices.

Strategies for Maintaining Resilience and Well-Being

Self-Care Practices Incorporating self-care practices such as regular exercise, mindfulness, and hobbies can help manage stress and improve mental health. Activities that promote relaxation and mental well-being, such as yoga or meditation, can be particularly beneficial.

Building a Support System Surrounding oneself with supportive friends, family, and colleagues can provide emotional stability and encouragement. Whistleblowers must communicate openly with their loved ones, ensuring they understand the challenges being faced and can offer appropriate support.

Seeking Legal Advice Consulting with legal

professionals who specialize in whistleblower cases can provide clarity and support in navigating legal challenges, although expensive and hard to retain. Having a solid legal strategy can alleviate some of the stress associated with the process and improve the chances of a favorable outcome.

The Importance of Self-Care and Asking for Help

One of the most crucial aspects of maintaining well-being during the whistleblowing process is recognizing the importance of self-care and the willingness to ask for help when needed. This is a process most fail to realize until it is too late.

Recognizing Burnout Whistleblowers must be aware of the signs of burnout, such as chronic fatigue, emotional exhaustion, and a sense of helplessness. Early recognition of these symptoms is key to addressing them before they become debilitating.

Reaching Out for Help Asking for help is not a sign of weakness but rather a crucial step in maintaining one's mental and emotional health. Even if it is to seek professional counseling, confide in a trusted friend. Maybe joining a local support group and reaching out can provide the necessary support to navigate your challenges of whistleblowing.

Creating a Routine Establishing a must and needed routine should include time for relaxation, exercise, and social interactions will help mitigate these stresses and provide a sense of normalcy during tumultuous times.

Conclusion

Managing one's emotional and psychological impact of whistleblowing is crucial for maintaining resilience and well-being. Access to psychological support, engaging with support networks, adopting self-care practices, and recognizing the importance of asking for help are all essential strategies that can help whistleblowers navigate their journey and continue their fight for justice.

Notes:

Chapter 7: Policy Recommendations and Future Directions

Enhancing Legal Protections

Enhancing legal protections for whistleblowers through amendments to existing laws and the introduction of new legislation can provide more robust safeguards. For instance, increasing the financial compensation available to whistleblowers, improving access to legal resources, and ensuring faster resolution of cases are essential steps in protecting these individuals from the unjust repercussions they often face.

Increasing Transparency

Encouraging Transparency within the VA by publicly acknowledging whistleblower contributions and ensuring accountability can build trust and encourage more individuals to come forward if done correctly. This could

Include creating public reports on the outcomes of whistleblower cases and recognizing whistleblowers who have made significant contributions to improving the VA system.

Improving the OAWP

Addressing the limitations of the OAWP by increasing staffing, funding, and streamlining processes can enhance its effectiveness and support for whistleblowers. This could involve setting up independent review panels to assess the OAWP's decisions and ensure that whistleblowers have access to a clear, unbiased appeals process.

Future Directions for VA Policies and Practices

Creating a Whistleblower-Friendly Culture Fostering a culture that values whistleblowers as integral to the VA's mission of transparency and accountability can encourage more individuals to speak out without fear. This involves training leadership and

Staff on the importance of whistleblowing and ensuring that whistleblowers are treated with respect and dignity, including help from 3rd party resources with outside communication channels.

Implementing Comprehensive Training

Providing training for VA employees on whistleblower rights and protections can raise awareness and reduce instances of retaliation. This training should be mandatory for all staff and include practical scenarios demonstrating how to appropriately handle whistleblowing cases.

Establishing Independent Oversight

Mandating an independent oversight mechanism can ensure impartial investigations and build confidence in the whistleblowing process. This could include establishing an external body to review the actions of the OAWP and the VA's handling of whistleblower cases.

Concluding Thoughts on the Need for Systemic Change

Whistleblowers play a vital role in upholding integrity and accountability within the VA. Their courage in exposing wrongdoing deserves recognition and robust protection. By implementing these policy recommendations and fostering a supportive culture, the VA can ensure that whistleblowers are protected, their voices are heard, and systemic change is achieved for the betterment of all.

Notes:

Additional Author's Perspective

Reflecting on the Journey

When I decided to blow the whistle on the Department of Veterans Affairs (VA), I expected a complex journey, but the reality was far more challenging than I could have imagined. My attempts to seek help from the Merit Systems Protection Board (MSPB) and the Office of Special Counsel (OSC) yielded little to no response, leaving me feeling abandoned by the very entities designed to protect whistleblowers. The Office of General Counsel (OGC) actively tried to change the narrative, painting me in a negative light to discredit my claims.

Lessons Learned the VA's legal and administrative apparatus mobilized to push for a settlement that required me to drop all accusations against the department. This tactic is a common strategy to silence whistleblowers, forcing them into a corner where their only options are to accept a settlement or face potentially career-ending consequences. When I refused to settle, they intensified their efforts, stripping me of my job and resources, making it incredibly difficult to continue the fight without legal representation. However, finding a lawyer willing to take on the federal government is another monumental challenge. Many law firms avoid such cases due to low payouts, caps on recoverable amounts, and the prolonged time frames involved. This leaves whistleblowers like me at the mercy of a system designed to wear us down, where every channel for defense seems to loop back to the same decision-makers who initially retaliated against us.

The systemic issues within the VA's leadership are glaringly evident during Joint Commission inspections. It is common knowledge that efforts to clean up and present a compliant front only intensify just before these inspections, highlighting the superficial approach to address internal problems. This pattern of behavior underscores the improper leadership decisions that permeate the VA.

In my case, these improper decisions were not limited to bureaucratic maneuvers but extended to outright deception. Specific individuals within the VA actively refused to gather and present exculpatory information, instead providing misinformation to the attorneys involved in my case. This betrayal was not just professional but deeply personal, as it affected every aspect of my life.

The path forward is a tangled process; it became clear that all channels of defense led back to the same network of individuals within the VA. The isolation and lack of support were profound, making the already arduous journey even more daunting. The personal and professional repercussions were severe, but my resolve to fight for justice and transparency kept me moving forward despite the overwhelming odds.

The journey of a whistleblower within the VA is fraught with challenges, from retaliation to legal battles and professional ostracism. Yet, it is a path that must be treaded for the sake of integrity and the well-being of the veterans we serve. This book is a testament to that journey, highlighting the silent sacrifices made and the resilience required to stand against systemic injustice.

Notes:

References:

- U.S. Office of Special Counsel. (n.d.). Whistleblower Protection Act. Retrieved from OSC website.
- Merit Systems Protection Board. (2020). Annual Report. Retrieved from MSPB website.
- Veterans Affairs Handbook 5021. (2017). Employee/Management Relations. Retrieved from VA Publications.
- U.S. Government Accountability Office. (2018). VA Whistleblower Protection: Improved Recording of Concerns Could Enhance Oversight. Retrieved from GAO website.
- Office of Accountability and Whistleblower Protection (OAWP). (2021). Annual Report. Retrieved from OAWP Reports.
- Mitchell, K. (2015). "Testimony before the U.S. House Committee on Veterans' Affairs." Hearing on Veterans' Health Care Delays at the Phoenix VA, April 2015.

- Coleman, B. (2016). NBC News Interview: "Whistleblower Exposes Issues in VA Suicidal Veteran Care," March 2016.
- Pedene, P. (2014). "Testimony on VA Financial Mismanagement," Senate Veterans' Affairs Committee Hearing, June 2014.
- Colon, J. (2015). "VA Whistleblower Suspended for Reporting Mismanagement," Government Accountability Office (GAO) Report on VA Retaliation, August 2015.
- Fox, J. (2017). "Unsafe Patient Care at Cincinnati VA: Whistleblower's Account," NBC News, March 2017.

Before You Speak: The Hidden Costs of Whistleblowing Against the Department of Veterans Affairs

By D.M.

Copyright © 2024 by D.M. All rights reserved.

www.ingramcontent.com/pod-product-compliance
Lightning Source LLC
Chambersburg PA
CBHW070413230526
45471CB00006B/2783